IT'S TIME TO EAT OKRA AND TOMATOES

It's Time to Eat OKRA AND TOMATOES

Walter the Educator

Silent King Books
A WhichHead Entertainment Imprint

Copyright © 2024 by Walter the Educator

All rights reserved. No part of this book may be reproduced in any manner whatsoever without written per- mission except in the case of brief quotations embodied in critical articles and reviews.

First Printing, 2024

Disclaimer

This book is a literary work; the story is not about specific persons, locations, situations, and/or circumstances unless mentioned in a historical context. Any resemblance to real persons, locations, situations, and/or circumstances is coincidental. This book is for entertainment and informational purposes only. The author and publisher offer this information without warranties expressed or implied. No matter the grounds, neither the author nor the publisher will be accountable for any losses, injuries, or other damages caused by the reader's use of this book. The use of this book acknowledges an understanding and acceptance of this disclaimer.

It's Time to Eat OKRA AND TOMATOES is a collectible early learning book by Walter the Educator suitable for all ages belonging to Walter the Educator's Time to Eat Book Series. Collect more books at WaltertheEducator.com

USE THE EXTRA SPACE TO TAKE NOTES AND DOCUMENT YOUR MEMORIES

OKRA AND TOMATOES

Come to the table, it's time to eat,

It's Time to Eat
Okra and Tomatoes

A dish that's healthy and so sweet!

Okra and tomatoes, fresh and bright,

A yummy meal that feels just right.

The okra's green, so smooth and long,

It makes this dish both bold and strong.

The tomatoes red, so juicy and round,

Their tangy taste is the best around.

Sizzle, sizzle, in the pan,

Cooking veggies, that's the plan.

A sprinkle of spices, a pinch of care,

Love is the secret hiding there!

Take a bite, oh what a treat,

The flavors dance, they can't be beat!

Soft and tender, warm and true,

Okra and tomatoes, just for you!

It's Time to Eat
Okra
and
Tomatoes

"Why is okra slimy?" some might say,

But that's the magic in its way.

It's fun to eat, so give it a try,

This special veggie will never lie!

Tomatoes bring a little zest,

In every dish, they are the best.

With every bite, you'll feel so strong,

Okra and tomatoes, can't go wrong!

This dish is packed with all things nice,

Healthy veggies, seasoned spice.

It makes us smile, it makes us grow,

A tasty meal, as we all know!

So let's say thank you, loud and clear,

For this yummy food we have right here.

Okra and tomatoes, a perfect pair,

It's Time to Eat
Okra
and
Tomatoes

A dish that shows how much we care.

Take another bite, enjoy the fun,

Our mealtime journey's just begun!

Okra and tomatoes, hip hooray,

A dish to brighten up our day!

When our plates are clean and done,

We'll say, "This meal was number one!"

Okra and tomatoes, always a treat,

It's Time to Eat
Okra
and
Tomatoes

A dish so simple and so sweet!

ABOUT THE CREATOR

Walter the Educator is one of the pseudonyms for Walter Anderson. Formally educated in Chemistry, Business, and Education, he is an educator, an author, a diverse entrepreneur, and he is the son of a disabled war veteran. "Walter the Educator" shares his time between educating and creating. He holds interests and owns several creative projects that entertain, enlighten, enhance, and educate, hoping to inspire and motivate you. Follow, find new works, and stay up to date with Walter the Educator™

at WaltertheEducator.com

www.ingramcontent.com/pod-product-compliance
Lightning Source LLC
LaVergne TN
LVHW052013060526
838201LV00059B/4015